To all the children in the world,
to share, respect, and enjoy
other cultures

WORLD MAP

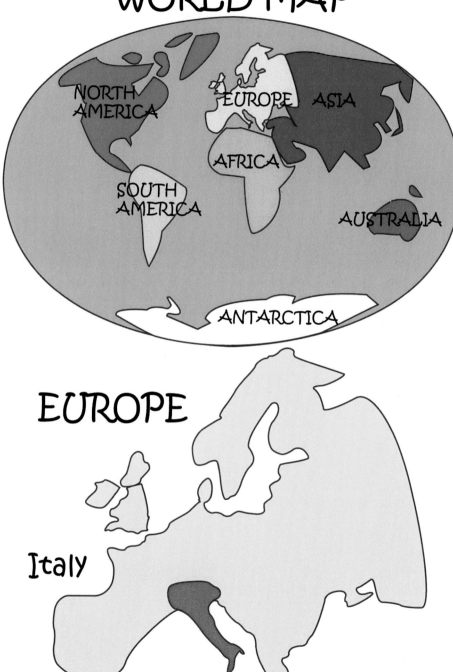

NORTH AMERICA

EUROPE

ASIA

AFRICA

SOUTH AMERICA

AUSTRALIA

ANTARCTICA

EUROPE

Italy

You Are Invited

to the Vatican

Aria was invited to a singing competition in Italy.
The winning choir would sing for the Pope.

Aria and Daisy were excited to travel to Rome,
which is the capital of Italy.

Aria's choir went to a restaurant after practice.
Aria and Daisy liked Italian food,
especially pasta and pizza.

The pizza chef said "Buongiorno" to everyone
and showed them how to toss pizza dough.
He then asked for a volunteer to try.

Aria raised her hand to try.

The dough almost touched the ceiling.

The pizza dropped and landed on Aria's head!
Everybody laughed.

Each morning the choir practiced singing.
They went sightseeing in the afternoons.

Aria and Daisy visited the Sistine Chapel.
They marveled at the paintings inside.

Outside the Sistine Chapel, kids from the choir
were amazed by the paintings inside.
They thanked the tour guide, "Grazie."

The Sistine Chapel tour guide said
"These paintings are a mystery.
Some say they are a map to all of Italy."

Aria thought she could make out
a map from the art.

The next day a choir member
did not show up for the practice.

Aria, Daisy, and other choir members
visited the Colosseum after the practice.
Aria noticed a sheet of music on the doorway.

They ate delicious gelatos
while walking around the Colosseum.
Gelatos tasted even better than ice-cream!
Unbelievable!

The next morning
more choir members went missing.
The teacher thought this was a true mystery.

In her friends' rooms,
Aria found train ticket receipts to Venice and Pisa.
Maybe that is where they went, Aria thought.

Aria and Daisy took a train to Venice,
a city built on water.

Aria and Daisy saw some kids looking familiar getting on a gondola.

One of them was holding a sheet of music.

Aria and Daisy took a gondola also
to follow them.

Aria asked the gondola driver to go faster,
but the other kids' gondola
raced away in the busy Grand Canal.

Aria and Daisy took a train to Florence,
then rode a bike through Tuscany.
Daisy saw a sheet of music in between flowers.

Aria and Daisy saw the same familiar looking kids near the Leaning Tower of Pisa.

Aria told them everyone was worried they were
missing and they must go back to Rome.
They said goodbye "Ciao"
to their Italian friends they met on the way.
They realized that the music sheets found
along the way were an ancient song.

When the teacher saw the missing kids were found,
she was relieved and happy
they were safe and sound.

Aria and the choir practiced the song they discovered.
They worked hard since there were only
a few days left to practice.

Finally, the day of competition came.
Several competing choirs sang beautifully.
The judges had a difficult time choosing the winner.

Aria's choir had won!
The judges had never heard
such a wonderful song before!

Everyone was surprised the Pope came
to congratulate them.
"Bravo!" said the Pope.

After the concert, Aria and Daisy visited
the Trevi Fountain and tossed a coin over
their left shoulders, to ensure a return to Rome.

Other Books by Anna Kim:

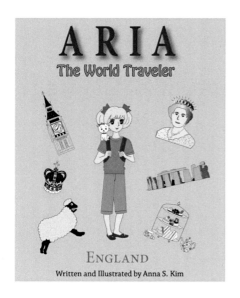

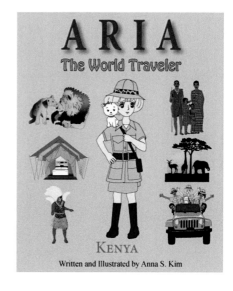

Other Books by Anna Kim (continued):

Pronunciation Guideline

Buongiorno: Boo-on-Jor-no

Grazie: Gr-Ah-zi-eh

Ciao: Cha-o

Made in the USA
San Bernardino, CA
26 November 2018